# MY MUSIC –
# MY BUSINESS:

## THE ULTIMATE GUIDE TO
## BUILDING INCOME FROM
## PLAYLISTING & STREAMING

*Or*

*How to Succeed in The Midst of The Music Streaming
Revolution*

### by Tim Sivers

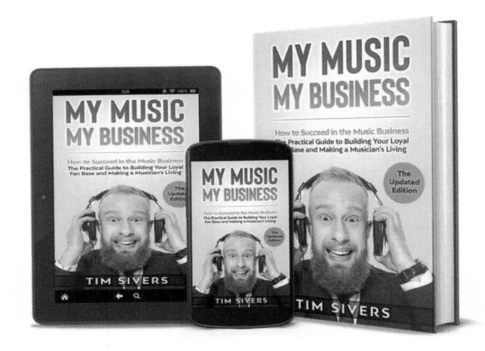

# BONUS

*As a special **THANK YOU** for your purchase, I have prepared a very special present for you.*

*I would like to offer you the 1ST book in the "My Music – My Business" series absolutely for **FREE**.*

*The link to your electronic copy you may find in the very end of this book.*

# TABLE OF CONTENTS

INTRODUCTION.............................................................. 10

CHAPTER 1 - STREAMING REVOLUTION: PAST, PRESENT, AND FUTURE.............................................. 14

A BRIEF HISTORY OF THE DIGITAL STREAMING REVOLUTION
............................................................................ 14

AN OVERVIEW OF DIGITAL STREAMING PROVIDERS...... 18

Spotify .............................................................................19

Apple Music .......................................................................21

TIDAL ..............................................................................22

Amazon ............................................................................22

Deezer .............................................................................23

Google Play........................................................................23

Pandora ...........................................................................24

YouTube ...........................................................................24

Others..............................................................................25

DIGITAL MUSIC DISTRIBUTORS AND HOW THEY OPERATE25

How do music distributors make money .........................................27

Overview of Digital Music Distributors..........................................28

CHAPTER 2 - THE POWER OF PLAYLISTS ............. 31

UNDERSTANDING THE POWER OF PLAYLISTS: INTRODUCTION ................................................................ 31

THE ROLE OF PLAYLISTS FOR EACH DIGITAL STREAMING SERVICE ............................................................ 34

Spotify ........................................................................35

Apple Music ...............................................................38

Pandora ......................................................................39

Soundcloud..................................................................39

CHAPTER 3 - BECOMING PART OF THE STREAMING REVOLUTION .............................................. 42

OVERVIEW OF THE PROPOSED MUSIC RELEASE STRATEGY42

Recording Strategy.....................................................43

Distribution ...............................................................44

Marketing & Advertising ...........................................45

Come Up with Your Playlist Plan of Attack.................45

Get a Digital Press Kit Made ......................................46

CHAPTER 4 - RECORDING: WHAT TO RELEASE IF YOU WANT TO GET ON PLAYLISTS ....................... 49

MARKET NICHES ............................................... 49

FOCUS ON SINGLES VERSUS ALBUMS........................... 51

THE STREAMING MUSIC ERA HIT SINGLES AND THEIR SUCCESS FORMULA........................................... 53

CHAPTER 5 - DISTRIBUTION ............... 57

TYPICAL REQUIREMENTS............................... 58

LEAD TIMES ..................................................... 59

## CHAPTER 6 - MARKETING / ADVERTISING CAMPAIGN ........................ 63

### GENERAL ELEMENTS OF PROMOTION ........... 64

Website ...................................................................64

Social Media .............................................................67

Fellow Artists ...........................................................68

Local Radio ..............................................................69

### COLLABORATIONS ......................................... 69

### MUSIC BLOGGERS, VLOGGERS & HOSTS OF MUSIC PODCASTS ........................................................... 71

### LOCAL COLLEGE RADIO .............................. 74

### PLAYLIST CURATORS ................................... 75

### HOW TO CHOOSE PLAYLISTS ................... 78

Your Own Curated Playlist ........................................79

## CHAPTER 7 - TRACKING OF RESULTS ............ 82

Where to Get Your Data: Information Sources .............83

### WHAT TO TRACK ........................................ 84

Playlists and Playlist Rankings ..................................84

Streams and Other Related Metrics ............................87

Soundcloud Followers ...............................................89

A Shazam ID & Shazam Spikes ...................................90

Audience Density in A Given Locale ...........................91

Artist Profile ............................................................92

Uploads to YouTube ..................................................92

Physical & Digital Purchases ....................................93

Traditional Radio Airplay .........................................94

Sync Deals ...............................................................94

*Music Bloggers* ............................................................... *95*

*Beatport* .......................................................................... *95*

## CHAPTER 8 - REALITY CHECK – CAN STREAMING REPLACE OTHER SOURCES OF INCOME? ............ 98

## CHAPTER 9 - THE FUTURE OF STREAMING AND YOUR STREAMING RELEASE STRATEGIES ....... 103

*Streaming Services = Record Companies* ..................................... *103*

*Exclusive Deals for Streaming Stars* ........................................... *104*

*The Rise and Fall Of Streaming Services* ..................................... *105*

*Smart Speakers and Playlists* ...................................................... *105*

## CONCLUSION .............................................................. 108

## BONUS ........................................................................... 111

# INTRODUCTION

W hen I was preparing to write this book, I thought a lot about one paradox in today's music industry. From one hand you have such major business publications as Forbes Magazine announcing the *streaming revolution* and that it has completely *taken over* the music industry. And from another hand – in reality, both the artists and music service providers are having a really difficult time generating enough income from this new form of music delivery.

Why is that? I believe it's because of the speed with which this music streaming revolution has evolved. There is still a lot of vagueness surrounding it. Not only beginning artists, but also seasoned musicians have a real need in a guide that will finally explain the world of music streaming and how to make the most of it.

My book is geared towards a wide audience – musicians and artists who are new to the music industry, up and comers, and even veterans. In other words, everybody who wants to learn more about becoming a digital musical success. I really hope that my book will help you get closer to this goal.

What can you expect from this book? We will cover a lot - the *streaming revolution*'s past, present, and future including an overview of digital streaming providers and digital music distributors, the role and importance of playlists for each digital streaming service.

We will of course discuss in detail how you can become part of the digital streaming revolution. I will cover recording, distribution, marketing, ad campaigns, and tracking your results. You will find out if streaming can replace other sources of income and finally we will talk about the future of music streaming and the trends you have to pay attention to.

I really would like you to enjoy this book and if you happen to have any feedback – please, do not hesitate to leave a few words with your impressions on Amazon. I am extremely grateful for your feedback and will also gladly take your advice for potential future subjects of **"MY MUSIC – MY BUSINESS"** series.

You can reach me at: *tim@musicmybusiness.com*

Thank you!

\* \* \*

*TIM SIVERS*

# CHAPTER 1

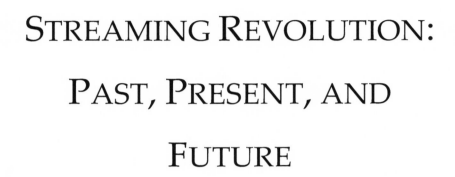

# STREAMING REVOLUTION: PAST, PRESENT, AND FUTURE

## A BRIEF HISTORY OF THE DIGITAL STREAMING REVOLUTION

Music streaming is a relatively new part of the music business. However as a means of acquiring and listening music it has very quickly replaced MP3s, which were considered to be the *"hottest"* development in music listening only a decade ago. Before the advent of music streaming, music providers placed songs and albums on their sites and made them available for download in the form of MP3, WMA, FLAC, or another form of audio file. Streaming eliminated the need to download and save files to your device; instead, music can now be simply 'streamed'. I.e. played directly from the streaming service on your device.

Streaming has definitely caught on as a way of music delivery and consumption. From 2014 to 2016, there was an estimated 66% increase of the music streaming market. In fact, it is estimated that Americans listened to approximately 32 hours of streaming music a week in 2017 and that has definitely risen since then. According to Billboard.com, a music industry information leader, on-demand streamed music topped 901 billion in 2018.

And consumers are definitely happy with this new way of consuming music that keeps the amount of money that they must spend low. Artists, on the other hand, have had complaints that they feel that they are virtually giving their music *"away"*. And even though they are compensated for the number of plays that their songs receive, some artists have been extremely dissatisfied by the amount of revenue generated by music streaming service royalties. The most notorious example of this dissatisfaction is *Taylor Swift* who has gone so far as to remove her music from streaming services before releasing her hit album "1989" in 2014.

So, how exactly does streaming music work? As I mentioned earlier, streaming music is a means of delivering music from a service provider that does not require the user/listener to download any files from the internet onto his or her computer or other receiving devices. Instead, after you connect to a streaming service and pass the required account verification, small packets of audio file data are delivered to your device allowing you to hear music. Music streaming is provided by music streaming services which include Spotify, Pandora, Apple Music, Deezer etc.

The way in which profit is made with music streaming differs from past forms of providing music such as MP3s, CDs, tapes, and records. These past forms of music consumption required the end user to purchase the individual music that he or she wanted to listen to. Music companies kept track of the sales of each article of music for the artist who was in turn compensated for the volume of purchases of his or her music. The music stores, either physical or online, retained a percentage of the purchase price.

With music streaming, however, music is no longer *"purchased"* individually. In order to make money, music streaming service providers allow their consumers to purchase a <u>subscription</u> to their service in order to make money. These music streaming services also make money from advertisements that they play. For this reason, many streaming services allow you to utilize the service for free, albeit not with all of the features that come with the paid subscription service and there are often a number of intrusive advertisements that are placed in between songs to allow the streaming service to collect advertising dollars.

One new way that artists, at least those with a huge following have been able to make money with streaming services recently is with exclusive releases. Big name artists sign deals with streaming music providers for the release of tracks exclusively on that service provider's platform. One example of this is the deal that *Chance the Rapper* signed with Apple Music for $500,000 to release music exclusively on that platform for 2 weeks in 2017. Another example is *Jay-Z* – the rapper owns a streaming service TIDAL, which he often uses for exclusive releases.

# An Overview of Digital Streaming Providers

There are a number of different digital service providers who are in the music streaming game. Digital service providers compensate artists for the number of plays of streams their songs receive at different rates. There is unfortunately not enough reliable payout statistics available for public access. However according to a 2017 Forbes Magazine online article entitled *"What Do the Major Streaming Services Pay Per Stream,"* the digital service provider which compensated artists the most per play was Napster (formerly, Rhapsody), with a $0.0167 play out per play. Various sources confirmed this payout to be the highest in the end of 2018 as well. The second highest payout, according to the article, was made by TIDAL at $0.011 per play. Again, no major difference by the end of 2018 as well. The rest of the digital service providers on the list include Apple Music at $0.0064, Google Play at $0.0059, Deezer at $0.0056, Spotify at $0.0038, Pandora at $0.0011, and YouTube at $0.0006. It is important to note that these playouts, no matter how small, are paid to the *person* or *entity* that *holds the rights to the song*, not necessarily the artist; thus, payouts may be split between an artist, songwriter, producer, and a record label making it difficult for many artists to see a profit.

18

There are a number of different digital service providers, so let's review the key ones.

This is the biggest global music streaming service. Spotify is a Swedish company and it was estimated to be worth approximately $25 billion when it went public in 2018. The company first launched in 2008, and it currently offers users and subscribers free and premium music streaming services. Many recording artists, however, have taken issue with this digital streaming service for the amount of royalties that it pays artists. This streaming music service, which has about 52% of the market in the United States only pays approximately $0.00397 per play of an artist's song (or at least it did in mid-2018). This is an extremely low pay per stream compared to other streaming music services.

While some musicians may be unhappy about this pay rate, in reality the importance of being available for streaming on this platform is absolutely crucial. In 2014 *Taylor Swift* complained publically about the fact that streaming services like Spotify did not compensate artists fairly. She decided to pull back her catalog of music off the service. However already 3 years later the case was actually resolved with her putting the catalogue back to the streaming service.

Indeed, this digital service provider is a very powerful force in music streaming. The library of Spotify contains over 30 million songs, and the platform has both *curated and user-generated playlists* (more on types of playlists later in the book). Based on the company's latest available report, there are over 190 million active users, over 87 million of whom are actually paying subscribers. It is important to know the number of subscribers and the market share because even with a lower payout per play, *more users mean that an artist can get significantly more plays on this platform* than he or she can on a number of other music streaming service platforms. Therefore, making your music available on Spotify is absolutely crucial if you want to reach mass market success.

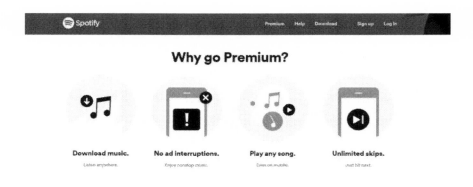

20

*Special Benefits for Artists*

Spotify is a very artist-friendly service to upload their music on so long as you ignore the low payout amounts. It allows the artist to put up and manage quite a detailed profile which serves as his or her homepage. This is where the artist can put up all of the information that he or she wants his fans to see: biography, pictures, links to the social media etc. The service provider even has deals set up with companies that will submit your music and collect your royalties so that you do not have to figure out how to do these things on your own. You can find more information and sign up for Spotify For Artists at https://artists.spotify.com/.

## APPLE MUSIC

Apple Music is considered to be the second most popular on-demand streaming service after Spotify. This service, unlike Spotify, is a purely subscription-based service which allows it to offer artists a much higher payout per play at $0.00783. This paid subscription only platform has garnered a significant percentage of the streaming music market share, with over 22% of the market utilizing this service. An interesting and popular feature of this digital music distributor is its hand curated live radio.

Apple Music has been actively utilizing celebrities for promotion of its service. *Drake*, who has an exclusive deal, as a promoter of Apple Music was rewarded greatly by the increased promotion of his songs on the streaming music platform. He became the highest streamed artists of 2018 with over 10 billion streams.

## *TIDAL*

TIDAL is a music streaming service that was started by *Jay-Z* and many of his heavyweight friends in the music industry. In 2018, this platform paid artists approximately $0.01284 per play, making it the second highest play per play platform for artists. However, at the same time the streaming service is generally known to have difficulties staying afloat due to rather slow growth of subscribers.

### *AMAZON*

Amazon provides two music streaming services, Amazon Prime and Amazon Music Unlimited. Although it is a well-known platform, it only has approximately 3.80% of the market between both streaming services. It pays artists around $0.0074 per play.

## DEEZER

Deezer is a French-based music streaming service which only has about 3.3% of the United States' market share. However, it is considered to be a powerhouse overseas, and it has a presence in 180 countries for artists who are not primarily interested in the US market. It pays approximately $0.00624 per play and offers more than 40 million songs on its platform.

## GOOGLE PLAY

For those of you who have heard that one of the main benefits of submitting to Google Play is their high payout per play, that benefit is no more. Although they used to compensate artists as much as $0.0179 per play, this payout has decreased significantly to approximately $0.00611 per play.

### Special Benefits for Artists

Google Play offers artists Artist hub so that the artist can decide how he or she wants to connect with his or her fans. You can offer subscribers traditional streaming music, live shows, or downloadable music. Unlike with the very low payout per stream, an artist can earn up to 70% of the retail price that the service suggests for music which is sold to fans instead of streamed. Furthermore, it is free to upload music onto the site.

## PANDORA

Surprisingly, Pandora, which is a very well-known music streaming service, has the 7.86% of the US market, giving it the third highest market share. Pandora has a very low payout for artists at approximately $0.00134 per play.

### Special Benefits for Artists

On Pandora, an artist can get his or her own station for free and use this station to reach millions of people worldwide. Generally, Pandora is an inexpensive way for you to build up a fan base.

## YOUTUBE

Another household name in music streaming, YouTube, only paid artists $0.00074 per play of the songs. Many would be surprised to find out that this digital service provider only controls 1.70% of the music streaming market in the United States. That said, in this case one has to differentiate *video streaming* and *audio streaming*. Based on a study conducted by Ipsos in 2017, YouTube attracted around 46% of *all music streaming listening time* in the world (excl. China). Clearly, the platform represents a very serious promotional resource for musicians. With a recent launch of its music only "YouTube Music" service, the position of YouTube in the music streaming business is only going to get stronger.

### OTHERS

One more notable digital streaming provider which I would like to mention here is *Soundcloud.* This service differs from many other streaming services in that it allows and promotes closer interactions between the artist and the fans. Artists can send individual fans music directly, and fans can offer comments on the music. It is important to note that you should not upload your music to Soundcloud directly if you would like to get paid for your music. You must go through such digital distributors as SongCast if you want to make money. One good thing about SoundCloud is that instead of having a set amount per play, you get paid a portion of the revenue generated that month based on your song plays compared to other artists on Soundcloud.

# DIGITAL MUSIC DISTRIBUTORS AND HOW THEY OPERATE

So, what is a digital distributor in the music streaming business? Digital distributors get your songs out to listeners by way of Spotify, Google Play, iTunes, and other streaming music platforms and digital music stores. They operate similarly to traditional distributors; however, they are distributing a *digital product* instead of a physical product (hence the name *digital* distributors).

There are a number of digital music distributors out there. I will list the biggest companies, but you should remember that this is a very competitive market and by the time when you read this book, some of these names may not exist/merge/acquire each other: CDBaby, TuneCore, DistroKid, Ditto Music, Symphonic, LANDR, MondoTunes, ReverbNation, RouteNote, The Orchard (labels only), AWAL (selected musicians only) etc.

The aforementioned digital distributors help you get your digital music to the platforms where it can be heard and even collect some of your royalties for you. They also make sure that your submissions are in the proper form so as not to hold up your release date. Many of these digital distributors work with different streaming music platforms and digital music stores, so you need to check out where they distribute compared to where you want your music your music to be before selecting a distributor.

## HOW DO MUSIC DISTRIBUTORS MAKE MONEY

Before we get to specific details about the conditions of distribution, let's take a look at the business model of digital distributors. A distributor typically earns money through asking their artists to pay a fee for adding an album or a single to their catalogue, by taking a certain percentage of royalties or by using a combination of these two approaches.

For most distributors who operate using the "distributor's fee" model, this fee is around ~10$ for a single (one song only) or around ~40$ for an album. In terms of average royalty percentage, the distributor's cut is typically around 10%. Some distributors also take annual fees to keep the content in their system. Typically, it's around 10-20$.

Why would an additional annual charge exist, you may ask? The reason for such a charge is protection against the situation when an artist stays relatively undiscovered, his/her music doesn't sell or doesn't get streamed often. In such situations neither the streaming service, nor the distributor are able to make money. Yet, the distributors do incur certain costs and have to protect themselves from such situations.

## OVERVIEW OF DIGITAL MUSIC DISTRIBUTORS

Given that every digital distributor offers unique partnership conditions, I decided to not list these conditions separately, but instead prepared a simple table, which covers only the most important partnership details for the biggest music distributors. Please, note that this table represents only current (beginning of 2019) information about the distribution conditions. These conditions change relatively often, depending on the market conditions/promotional campaigns etc.

| | CDBABY | DISTRO KID | TUNE CORE | DITTO MUSIC |
|---|---|---|---|---|
| DISTRIBU- TION FEE PER SINGLE | 9,95$ | No fee, unlimited | 9.99$ | No fee, unlimited |
| DISTRIBU- TION FEE PER ALBUM | 29-49$ (depends on promo) | No fee, unlimited | 29.99$ | No fee, unlimited |
| COMMIS- SION PER STREAM / SALE | 9% | 0% | 0% | 0% |
| ANNUAL FEE | 0% | 19,99$ | 9.99$ per single 49.99$ per album | 19$ |
| WEBSITE / SPECIAL SIGN UP CONDITIONS | www. cdbaby. com | SPECIAL 7% DISCOUNT www. distrokid. com/vip/ seven/ 736485 | www. tunecore. com | www. dittomusic. com |

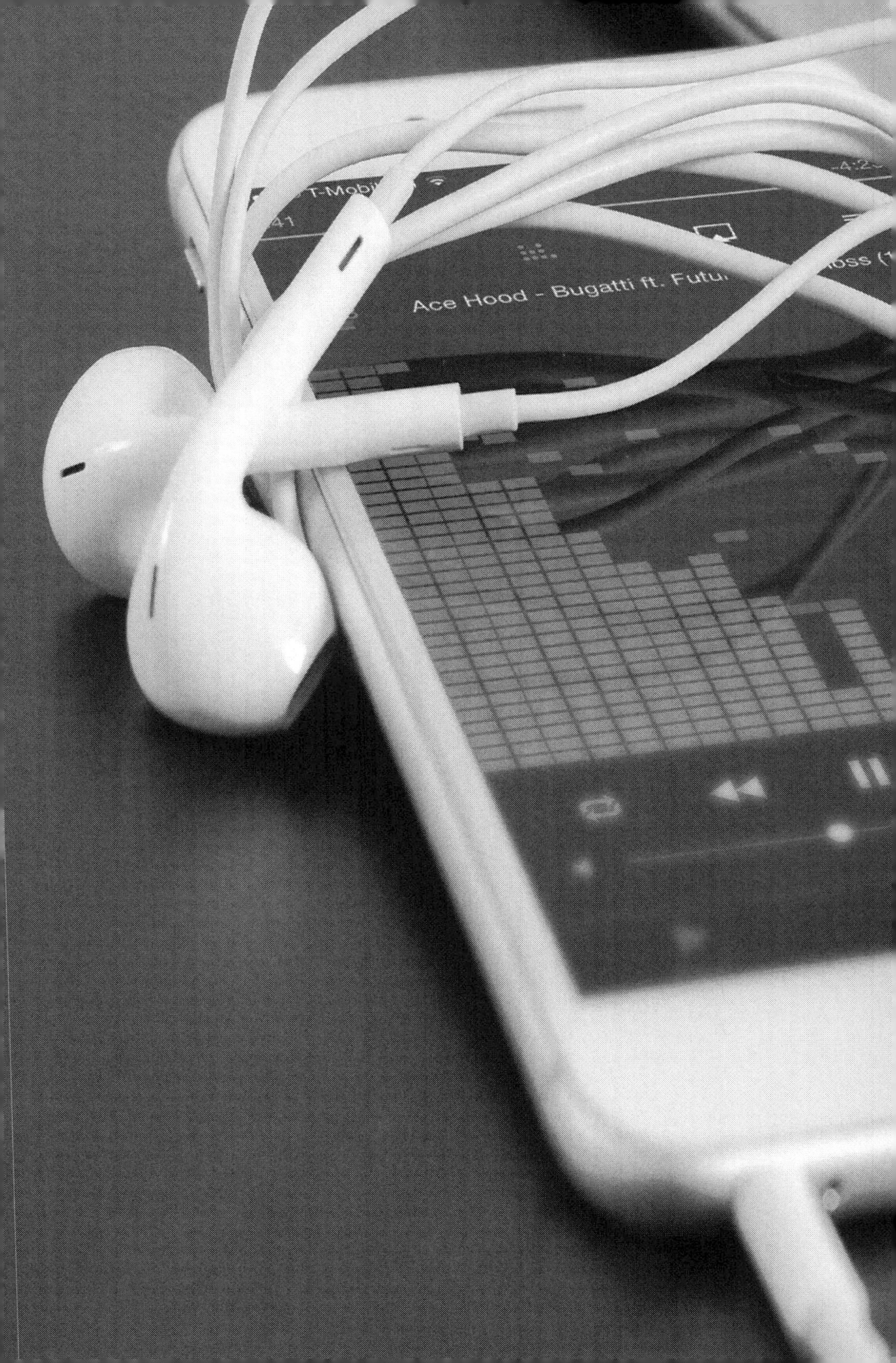
Ace Hood - Bugatti ft.

# CHAPTER 2

# THE POWER OF PLAYLISTS

## UNDERSTANDING THE POWER OF PLAYLISTS: INTRODUCTION

Playlists are one of the primary ways that people listen to music on streaming music services. According to Pitchfork, 31% of listeners listen to playlists as opposed to 29% who listen to albums. Among the younger audience this split is even more noticeable – 45% mainly listen to playlists, while 31% mainly listen to albums. Thus, getting on a '*hot*' playlist should be a very important part of music promotion for any artist.

Streaming music services pay artists per play or stream of their songs; therefore, it is essential for artists, especially artists that are not household names, to get on playlists in order to get their songs heard and played more often. In fact, the more popular the playlist that an artist gets on, the more money that he or she can expect to make.

Getting on a playlist can pluck your song out of a music library filled with 40 million songs and get it in front of listeners. This is extremely important for new and up and coming artists who may not be able to drive a large number of people specifically to their songs.

## THE TYPES OF PLAYLISTS AND HOW THEY WORK

### Streaming Service Playlists

These playlists are created by streaming services and are typically well researched and tuned to satisfy all possible individual's tastes. Typically, in streaming service playlists similar songs are grouped together based on a ***similar music genre, category, mood or occasion of music consumption***.

Users of the streaming service cannot change anything in these playlists, however they can copy the playlists, make them their own and then make changes to them. Moreover, on many of the streaming music services, if a listener hears your song in a streaming service playlist and likes the song, he or she can add it to his or her own personal playlist of songs the listener listens to regularly. This is generally considered a crucial part of the music promotion efforts, as you would like as many people as possible to add you to their personal playlist.

I would also like to add a few words about *mood and occasion of music consumption playlists*. These playlists are created by the streaming services for specific moods (*sad, depressive, happy songs* etc) or activities (such as *working out, driving, showering* etc). Such types of playlists may be accessed by a large number of listeners who are engaging in this activity or even businesses such as gyms. There may even exist some niche playlists inside a particular activity. For instance, the *workout* playlist category is so popular that Spotify has a *Runner* playlist specifically for listeners who are running as their form of working out. Thus, when thinking of activities which your music might be associated with, it is better to be as specific as possible and select all playlists, even from the sub-niches, which might be suitable. This will increase your chances of getting on such playlists.

Another great advantage about mood or occasion based music listening playlists is the fact that they are often used by music supervisors when selecting songs for sync placement. This is a great way to start earning money not only from streaming but also from licensing your music for television shows, films, games, advertising etc.

*Branded Playlists*

Branded playlists are just what they sound like, playlists run by brands. Some record companies and other music industry giants have playlists. Typically, unless you're associated with a certain brand or a company, it's quite difficult to get featured on such a playlist.

*Personal / collaborative playlists*

This is the kind of playlists which users of each streaming platform create on their own or together. While there are many personal playlists, which are unknown, undiscovered and have a really small number of followers, some personal playlists may be quite popular and sometimes can compete in popularity even with the streaming service curated playlists.

# THE ROLE OF PLAYLISTS FOR EACH DIGITAL STREAMING SERVICE

Playlists are central to how streaming music services operate, and all of them use the playlist in much the same way. To stay ahead of the curve some of the streaming services are trying to come up with unique twists on playlists; however, they all offer many of the same elements in playlist features.

## SPOTIFY

### Curated (Editorial) Playlists

This music streaming service offers curated playlists upon which music chosen by their in-house editorial staff appear. A few examples of a Spotify curated playlists include *Rap Caviar, Hot Country, Rock Classics, Peaceful Piano, Sleep, Deep Focus* etc. These Spotify playlists have literally millions of followers and receive tremendous promotion across the platform. To get on these types of playlists as a newbie, you need to either have a mega-hit or have some strong connections in the industry. A great publicist or digital promotions expert can help, however these services do require significant budget. Recently, Spotify made it easier to get on one of their editorial playlists without spending additional money. Simply go to your *Spotify For Artists* account (typically, the access is provided by your digital distributor), select one <u>unreleased</u> song from a future release, fill out a small questionnaire about yourself/your music and submit it for playlist consideration.

35

*Algorithmic Playlists*

The most well-known algorithmic playlists are called *Release Radar* and *Discover Weekly*. They are called algorithmic because they are automatically populated by Spotify. *Release Radar* is simply a compilation of new songs from the artists which you interacted with on Spotify. *Discover Weekly* has a more interesting concept – the songs are chosen based on your past listening habits as well as the habits of other users with similar music tastes.

While it may seem to you that these algorithmic playlists are not as useful for music promotion compared to the editorial Spotify playlists, in reality it isn't so. According to industry experts, algorithmic playlists may be very useful especially for new and up and coming artists due to the following reasons:

1) Songs on these playlists actually get a lot of plays (=royalties),

2) Successful songs on these playlists may be selected for curated playlists.

*Personal Playlists*

There are two types of personal playlists, *your own* and *other people*'s. It may not seem like that big of a deal to be on your own playlist, but *it is* if you promote it. In fact, if you get a significant number of followers to your personal playlist, all of your music will receive more plays. To promote your playlist, you need to place them prominently on your social media sites. And make sure that your playlists feature a lot of great music from other artists to draw followers to the playlist (*It may be hard to drive followers to a playlist which only features one artist's music no matter how good the music is.*).

In addition, you want to try to get your music on *other people's playlists*, especially playlists with a bunch of followers. One really simple way to find a lot of popular personal Spotify playlists is to type something like '*Spotify Rap Playlist*' into the Google search bar. The next step is to follow the playlists you want to be included in, contact the list owners and ask to have your song added. If your request is honored, it's a good idea to encourage your followers to follow that playlist, so that the list owner would honor similar requests from you in the future.

*Collaborative Playlist*

A collaborative playlist is one that can be altered by any of the followers who can add and delete songs. This is an interactive playlist which allows followers to feel as if they are part of making the playlist great. You should try to add your song to some collaborative playlists that already have followers.

*Some additional thoughts about playlists on Spotify*

For an artist to get on playlists on Spotify, it is important for him or her to put up a profile and stay active on the platform. It is especially important for your profile to be verified. Only recently Spotify required that you have a minimum of 250 followers before your profile can be verified. Luckily, this requirement is no longer relevant. This change came with opening *'Spotify For Artists'* portal on their website, which signified a new stage in development of artist/streaming service relationships.

## APPLE MUSIC

While being the 2nd largest streaming service, Apple Music does not have such an extensive network of playlists as we've just seen with Spotify. Yet, the basic functionality in terms of playlists is of course available.

The service offers curated, private and shared playlists. According to available statistics, the overwhelming majority of users, an estimated 9 out of 10, have created playlists and more than half of the streaming music platform's subscribers listen to one of these playlists every time they use the service.

38

Of the curated playlists, the *'Top Hits'* lists are the most popular of the playlists that the users listen to; these playlists are normally separated out by genre. In fact, 29% of users listen to *Today's Hits* every time they tune in to the streaming music service. The *Discovery Mix* is also a playlist that approximately 44% of users listen to. And the *A-List: Hip Hop* is a playlist that has made a number of stars and is comparable to *Rap Caviar* from Spotify.

One good thing about playlists on Apple Music is that they are sharable, and many people create playlists and then share them with their friends and family.

## PANDORA

It is interesting to note that all of the music streaming services use playlists for their paid and free tiers if they have one except Pandora. Pandora does not offer playlists to its free subscribers and considers playlists to be for its premium members only.

## SOUNDCLOUD

This streaming music service allows artists to upload their own tunes as either singles or playlists (As stated earlier, do not upload to the site directly if you would like to make some money from having your tunes on SoundCloud.)

SoundCloud offers listeners a chance to interact more with the artist, so you would be wise to interact with listeners and ask them what songs of yours you should include on your playlist along with what song by other artists would help to round out the list.

# CHAPTER 3

# BECOMING PART OF THE STREAMING REVOLUTION

N ow that you have learned about the streaming music providers, the distributors and you have gained some knowledge of playlists, the time has come to find out exactly *how* you can become part of the streaming revolution!

## OVERVIEW OF THE PROPOSED MUSIC RELEASE STRATEGY

A *strategic music release* can have a number of advantages over just simply uploading songs and hoping that they will catch on as far as building some traction and gaining fans is concerned.

The key steps of a strategic music release are the following:
- define your *recording strategy*;
- correctly choose your *distribution* service;
- plan your *marketing* & *advertising* campaign;
- *track your results / fine tune your campaign*

Now, I would like to offer a few important tips about the strategy of music releases. Then we will discuss each of the above-mentioned steps separately.

## RECORDING STRATEGY

If you do not have a lot of followers, my best advice is to attack a *niche market*. These smaller segments of the general population are less competitive, and your music is less likely to get lost in the sea of other songs. If there is anything that is unique about you or the music that you can exploit to build a fan base, go for it!

In addition, if you are an up and comer, you want to focus on having some hot catchy singles that will grab listeners attention as soon as possible. In the streaming music world listeners often skip songs, especially ones that they have never heard before, so your song has to be very catchy. For this reason, you should not simply concentrate on putting out *singles*, they should be _streaming music era singles_. More on that in the chapter about *recording*.

## DISTRIBUTION

Choose your distributor wisely. We will talk about this in the corresponding chapter, but you don't want your release to be 'stuck' or 'rejected' after the process of internal distributor's review because they have a notoriously bad record of accepting the style of music you produce.

It is important to ensure that your submissions follow the guidelines which are laid out by the streaming music services. Although they are generally pretty easy to find, it may be best (especially, if you are new to streaming music releases) to contact your digital distribution company and ask them for additional assistance. You will save a lot of time and potentially money by doing so!

Be sure to give yourself enough lead time so that all of your music is available on the platforms that you submitted it to by your set release date. The lead times vary somewhat depending on a distributor and the streaming platforms. So make sure you know which platforms take the most time and use that as your guide to how much in advance you need to have everything ready and submitted to hit a certain target release day.

## MARKETING & ADVERTISING

You need to *market, market, market* yourself and your music. Start by creating a professional website and having all of your social media accounts focused on your music and ready to go. Next, get in touch with fellow artists to try to join forces in promoting yourselves and each other. Try to get some collaborations with other artists. Contact local and college radio. Get in touch with music bloggers, podcasts hosts, and vloggers, even consider offering them an exclusive before your release if they will review or feature your work. And please, *do not stop* after your release is out – it's the time to get active!

## COME UP WITH YOUR PLAYLIST PLAN OF ATTACK

I highly recommend to come up with a targeted playlist plan of attack because being on a good playlist has so much to do with the success of your single. You can submit your song to the very well followed playlists but do not get your hopes up of getting on these playlists *"automatically"* until you have managed to generate some good buzz. Instead, try contacting *independent playlist owners* with a notable

45

following (use their social media). Ask them to have a listen and maybe include one or more of your songs on their playlist.

You also need to create your own playlists and try to get others to follow them. Specific tricks and techniques to build up a following for your playlists are outlined later in this book.

## GET A DIGITAL PRESS KIT MADE

One of the crucial element of your music release strategy should be to get a digital press kit made. This is what you may want to send out to bloggers, playlist curators, some fans, industry tastemakers, and anyone who can help to make your release a success. Your digital press kit should include your music, the genre that your music is in and comparisons to other artists and songs in that genre, a compelling signature story that will catch people's attention and pull them in, photos of yourself as well as album artwork, your website information, and links to your social networks. (Even though your website information is included in your press kit, you should upload your press kit with that information in it to your website.) You can hire a PR person to make you a digital press kit, do it yourself, or check out a site such as Ditto Music or ReverbNation.

(ReverbNation press kit guidance: https://www.reverbnation.com/band-promotion/press_kit). You can probably even get someone on *Fiverr* to build an electronic press kit for you for a very reasonable price.

# CHAPTER 4

# RECORDING: WHAT TO RELEASE IF YOU WANT TO GET ON PLAYLISTS

## MARKET NICHES

To get on a playlist which already has a significant number of followers, it may be important to try to target some market niches. For example, if you want to release a hip-hop song that may be added to a number of playlists, you may want to try releasing one that would make a great *workout* song because workout songs are a very popular targeted niche market. 'Have a Great Day' is one of the most popular Spotify playlists and it contains 100 songs that are positive and upbeat to encourage you to have a great day. In addition, *relaxation songs* are popular across a number of genres. Attacking smaller niche markets can help your song be directed toward more targeted playlist, and the owners of the list may be more interested in songs that seem '*made for*' the specific list.

Rap and Hip hop dominate the music streaming game according to Billboard.com. Almost all of the songs in the top ten most streamed songs of 2018 were in this genre of music. Thus, if you're a producer it would be most prudent to concentrate on exploiting market niches in this genre to maximize the likelihood that the song will receive a sufficient number of streams.

Furthermore, you shouldn't think that if you decide to attack a 'market niche', your audience size is going to be small. An artist can make money and build a sustainable career by attacking niche markets that seem like a small portion of their local region (say, moms who would like to play calm songs to their little children). However *all these numbers add up* when looking at the total number of such music listeners globally.

## Focus on Singles Versus Albums

One thing that streaming music has arguably done is to increase the focus on *singles* instead of *albums*. This is especially true for the younger artists according to Rolling Stone Magazine. Two typical examples of this, according to the renowned music magazine, are that of popular artists *Camila Cabello* and *Cardi B*. These artists put out six and four singles respectively before putting out their first album. Concentrating on putting out hot singles allowed these artists to see more commercial success *before* releasing an album which of course, in turn, helped them ensure high album sales. Other artists to follow the multiple single release trend include *Taylor Swift, Jason Derulo, Rae Sremmurd* according to "Why Your Favorite Artist Is Releasing More Singles Than Ever" (Leight, Elias, *Rolling Stone*). The magazine credits the effects of streaming and social media for a faster pace in the music industry which requires that artists constantly come out with new hot songs.

---

*Beyoncé, on the other hand, showed that a great single album release could put you on top of the streaming music game when she released "Lemonade" in 2016. There was only one single "Formation" which preceded the album and*

*was released exclusively on TIDAL. Of course,
Beyoncé is an exception here, since she was
already a mega-star, so fans expected to hear
more from her than just one hit song.*

---

Putting out singles also gives artists the chance to see which songs are doing well and that they should put their promotional efforts behind. An artist may think that a certain song will be popular, and it ends up not living up to par; thus, putting a few singles out on a streaming music service can help an artist decide which one to focus on.

There is also another aspect of releasing singles for indie artists. Because artists may feel the need to put out a number of hit singles that will receive significant streams before finally putting an album out, the total number of single releases may have a negative effect on the album. Fans may not get as excited about a new album with only a fewer new songs because half of the songs on the album have been on streaming music services for months before the album drops. Thus, many new and up and coming artists with songs on streaming music platforms may just want to focus on putting out singles and delay the release of an album until they have built up a significant following. Furthermore, artists may want to abstain from placing all of their singles on their newly released album. This may increase the interest and album value in the eyes of potential fans.

### THE STREAMING MUSIC ERA HIT SINGLES AND THEIR SUCCESS FORMULA

As I mentioned earlier, tracks, in today's streaming music world, need to have much shorter intros and get to the hook faster than they did in the past. This keeps listeners from jumping over the track to the next song.

To keep a song from being fast-forwarded over to the next song on a playlist, the song needs to get 'catchy' quickly. For this reason, many artists placing songs on streaming music platforms may choose to forgo an intro altogether. If you choose to include an intro, you definitely do not want it to be too long.

In fact, one reason that streaming media has been credited with changing the structure of songs that are being put out is that a significant number of artists are choosing to start their songs off with the chorus or hook. This gets the listener captivated on the catchiest part of the song immediately. One popular example of this is *Lil Uzi Vert*'s 2017 song "*The Way Life Goes,*" which both starts and ends with the chorus, lacks an intro, almost no instrumentals or big beat drops or even a bridge; the popular song is only about 3 minutes and 41 seconds long as well.

And it is not just to avoid being skipped over that tracks have become shorter. Some credit the fact that streaming music pays so little per stream as the reason that songs have been shortened. Remember the golden rule - songs pay **the same amount per stream whether they are long or short**; in fact, a play of **greater than 30 seconds is already considered 'payable'** and **it doesn't matter if a song is streamed longer afterwards**. Therefore, it makes sense to produce shorter songs which cause listeners to play your songs twice or more times in a row. There is a well calculated commercial reason why the 2017 hit song *Gucci Gang* is only 2 minutes and 4 seconds long!

It's already an established statistical fact that the length of songs, in general, has gotten shorter. In the past five years, songs have dropped in length approximately 20 seconds and currently average around 3 minutes and 30 seconds by the average artist whether he or she is an established artist or a new artist.

The one exception to putting out shorter songs is putting out 'soundtracks' to your music videos. Music streaming platforms don't just offer songs, they offer videos as well, and some recording artists are going all out with their videos to draw in listeners/viewers. This means that some tracks may not be suitable for the radio at all; in fact, you may not even understand the meaning of the some by simply listening to it. One example of this is the song "This is America" by *Childish Gambino*. The song goes along with the action in the video; even still, no matter how much action takes place in the video, the song is still only a little over 4 minutes long.

So, to sum up, try to pay attention to the following when deciding on your next single release:

- Avoid long intro and/or obscure beginning of your single
- Make sure that your chorus is either in the beginning of the track or that your first verse does not last excessively long. Remember, that music listeners on each music streaming service need only <u>one second</u> to click on the "next track" button!
- I would highly recommend that your total track length should not be significantly more than ~3 minutes
- Focus on creating a *series* of short catchy singles with a similar vibe that listeners will put on repeat.

# CHAPTER 5

# DISTRIBUTION

N ow that we have covered *what* you need to record to get your future playlist placement, let's discuss *how* to get your music to the music streaming service. Unless your music is managed by a music label, the best way to get your music to streaming providers is to go through a digital distributor. As I explained earlier, these distributors deal with the streaming music services all the time and can make sure that your submission meets all the requirements for file format and the like as well as ensure that your music is submitted with the proper lead time to guarantee that you make your release date.

# TYPICAL REQUIREMENTS

Every digital distributor have certain specs that a submission must meet. Typically they don't differ significantly, however it's helpful to know the key parameters:

*Audio*

The standard requirement is that your audio files must be in stereo and either WAV or FLAC format, 44.1 kHz sample rate, and 16 bit. Even though some distributors like DistroKid claim that they also accept MP3, AIFF, MP4 (M4A), WMA, in reality it's better to make sure you deliver the highest quality material from the beginning and avoid using compressed lossy audio files for building your music portfolio with the music streaming services. This is because some music services already offer high quality streaming plans for their subscribers, where music is delivered in high definition (TIDAL).

*Artwork*

Your cover art also needs to comply with very strict requirements. Your artwork should be at least 1400 x 1400 pixels, 72 – 3000 dpi, less than 25 mb, and with an RGB color scheme.

*Other Requirements*

In terms of additional requirements, your digital music distributor typically asks for:

- Songwriter and publisher information for each track;
- UPC barcode for your release (some provide it for free or sell it as additional service, e.g. CDBaby);
- ISRC codes for each of your songs (provided for free, if you don't have them)

The good news is that even if you are not familiar with this kind of stuff, there are helpful guides available on most of digital distributors' websites. And even if these requirements change over time, typically this sort of information tends to be clearly listed on the submission page, or there is a link to the information from the submission page.

# LEAD TIMES

If you have a certain release date that you want to meet, you must take into account the proper lead times so that all of your streaming channels have your music in time for the release. TuneCore suggests that you send your music to the digital distributor at least three weeks ahead of your scheduled release date. And if you wish to submit your song for playlist consideration to Spotify Editorial team, your track has to be delivered to Spotify at least seven days ahead of your release date.

Furthermore, it is very important that you check to make sure that the release meets all of the formatting guidelines that digital distributors clearly outline on the site in order to avoid delays in getting your music out. What this means is that if you do not have the technical skills and knowledge to do the formatting yourself, you want to pay somebody else to format your files. The good news is that you can probably find someone on Fiverr who can format the files for you for a very low price.

If you are unsure of whether or not your files have been formatted correctly, I would advise to get them to the distributor *in advance* of the recommended three weeks to find out whether any delays are going to or have occurred.

Just so that you know, here are some lead times for streaming music platforms and MP3 sites music stores. Please, note that typically digital distributors take from 1 to 5 business day to review your files. Afterwards, the files are sent to the streaming platforms and the lead times are managed by these streaming services.

- From the time you submit your music to **iTunes**, it can take up to 48 hours for the music to make it onto the platform and be released.

- **Spotify** can take up to five business days from the date that they receive your submission for it to be in the store on their site.

- **Amazon On Demand** may take 6 to 8 weeks; this is very important to note if you plan to submit music here.

- **Amazon Music**, however, would only take from 1 to 3 business days to get your songs on their platform.

- **Deezer** and **iHeartRadio** take up to seven business days to put your songs out in their stores.

- **Google Play** may take up to two weeks.

And once again, please do not forget that with most digital distributors you can set a future release date so that all of your music comes out in the stores *at the same time*.

# CHAPTER 6

## MARKETING /

## ADVERTISING CAMPAIGN

I f you do not already have a record deal and you are
trying to enter into the music business by uploading
your songs to streaming music services, promotion is
the *most important element of success* for you right behind
having talent. This is because you need to be your own
promoter unless you have the money to hire a good one. And
since you are not affiliated with a record company, there is a
good chance that you will not be able to get enough people
to listen to your music no matter how hot it is without a little
promotion.

# GENERAL ELEMENTS OF PROMOTION

## *WEBSITE*

This is 21st century and having a website is considered to be a basic foundation piece in promoting one's self these days. Everybody has one and people will wonder why they cannot find yours if you don't. Designing your website correctly and including all of the important information can be a great promotional tool that makes you look more professional. Please, do not think that a *Facebook/Instagram/Twitter pages* are your 'websites'. You really need to have your own dedicated space on the web.

One key feature of your website is that your music artist name should be in the domain. This will make it much easier for people to find your website. You can buy domains for around $10 a year or less on sites so make sure that you spend the extra money for this feature.

There are other elements that your website should include. Your website should include an *artist bio,* and you want to make it as catchy as possible. Skip the boring basic facts type of bio and tell a creative story about why or how you got into music that makes you stand out. Furthermore, if you have any unique interests, hobbies, or memberships that may draw in a group of similar people be sure to include that in the bio.

In addition, your bio should include a lot of action words as a passive bio just does not hook the reader as much. You may even want to include the motivation behind some of the some of the songs that you have on your site. Listeners may find it interesting to find out if the motivation behind a sad song was a *painful break-up,* something that you *saw in a movie,* or just a *creative expression* of your talent. Try to let fans 'in' as much as possible through your bio words and pictures so that they feel they are getting to know you; this will help to create more interest in you and your music.

Your website needs to have a *music player* that plays your best songs. Don't wait for someone to click on a link so that they can hear your songs. Have the music player out on the front page playing when someone enters your site.

It is also good to include any *video and pictures* of yourself that you think represent your music image/persona. Don't forget about the images which depict you performing your music either at your home or in a show.

It is very important to include a *subscribe feature* or an *email signup form* because you want to keep all of the visitors that you attract to your site. A typical mistake of indie musicians is to collect e-mails and never communicate with your subscribers. Try to send out a short newsletter every few months or so. If you have nothing to say, just include your upcoming concert and/or music release dates.

Also, be sure to include *links to all of your social media profiles, including Spotify "FOLLOW" button.* You can ask visitors of your website to like / follow you Spotify and on these social media channels. It is always good to be able to reach as many of your fans and followers as possible.

Speaking about the contact information - make sure to include your/your promoter's e-mail address or a website message form that a music industry professional that visits your site may be able to use to get in contact with you.

Lastly, your website needs to have a *music store* where people can buy copies of your music directly from your site. Even though we are living in the midst of the music streaming revolution, some people still prefer to support their favorite musicians directly.

A few words about your website design. There are many website design platforms available out there. However regardless of the platform, you need to make sure that your website is neat and professional so that it *stands out* from the proliferation of websites that are on the internet today. If you have the funds, I would advise to spend some money to have your website *professionally done*. A great looking website can give people the impression that you are a professional who is really trying to make it in the music industry instead of a hobbyist. This is especially important when you are trying to enter the music scene through streaming your own music because it gives the impression that you are a soon-to-be-discovered talent.

## SOCIAL MEDIA

Yes, you need to have a strong presence on social media even if you have a webpage. You should have links to your social media on your webpage, however, as I mentioned earlier do not neglect either the website or social media thinking that it is okay to have one or the other but not both.

You should make sure that your social media pages are primarily focused on you as an artist and not just regular social media pages. The people who click on the links from your website should still feel like they are checking out a music artist when they get to your social media pages, they are just delving deeper into you as a person as your musical aspirations. All of the important information from your website should be included in your social media profiles and pages. Try to add a little more information on these pages so that people will continue to check out both the website and follow you on social media.

## FELLOW ARTISTS

Fellow artists are a great avenue for promotion. No, you probably won't be able to get any big-name artists to back your work at first, but don't be discouraged. There are still many other ways to use fellow artists to promote your music. Try contacting other artists who are in a similar genre on *Spotify* or *SoundCloud* and see if you can get them to play your music on their playlists or comment about your songs and their quality.

In addition, you can try to contact local artists. Even famous local artists may be willing to meet with you to hear you sing. See if anyone is willing to give you an opportunity to sing as an opening act at one of their shows. In addition, local artists are a great networking tool, and they can introduce you to the music industry professionals in the area.

## Local Radio

Local radio shows are always a great promotional tool. Try going up to the radio station and singing for one of the DJs. They will often let you sing on the air if you do a great job; this is especially true if you have a professional website so that they can see that you are serious about your work. In addition, may want to send the radio a copy of your single and see if they will play it on the air.

# COLLABORATIONS

Collaborations are very important in the music industry and have helped to launch a number of careers for big-name artists. Yes, you want to do a collaboration with another artist if possible; this can be a great step in increasing your audience size and your number of followers. Connect with artists on some of the streaming music providers' platforms on which you plan to put your music to see if any of them are interested in a collaboration. You may want to try contacting them through the social media links on their artist page. If you are lucky, you may be able to convince an artist who already has a sufficient following and may even be on some playlists to do a collaboration with you. This may be one of the quickest ways to get yourself on a playlist if you are starting off.

However, even if you cannot get an artist who already has traction on that particular streaming music platform to agree to collaborate with you, someone who is just starting out is good too if you are new. If you put out a song with another person, you get your music in front of a large audience as the other person should draw in some listeners as well. And you have a chance of growing your followers by gaining some of theirs. You can ask your fellow collaborator to mention you on his or her social media pages and even provide a link to your website from his or her own.

If you are unable to find a fellow collaborator by contacting people who are already on the streaming music platform that you plan to submit your music to, you can attend local music events and introduce yourself to some of the performers to see if any of them would be open to collaboration. Maybe you will even get to do a live performance of two together, and you can upload the video your respective websites.

You can also collaborate with other artists on building a collaborative playlist. This would be a benefit to each member of the collaboration as the playlist would be in front of each of their group of followers. Contact a few artists who have similar music to yours to see if they want to start a collaborative playlist.

# MUSIC BLOGGERS, VLOGGERS & HOSTS OF MUSIC PODCASTS

When promoting your music it's extremely important to talk to the opinion leaders in the music world. You need to contact respected music bloggers who have a significant following and ask them to review your song; make sure that you have gotten enough positive feedback from others and tweaked out the imperfections before doing so. Music bloggers can bring a good bit of attention to your song if they like it and give it a good review; however, they can also give you the message that your song does not *measure up* or it is *not quite ready yet*. If you get a negative answer, do not get discouraged! Remember that you can't please all of the people all of the time. Plus, in some cases even a bad review can have some benefits as it still means extra exposure.

A good tactic to avoid negative reviews could be sharing an advanced copy before the song is released. This way you will know if you are going to receive a positive or negative review. This will at least give you the opportunity to make changes or decide if you want to release the song at all (if you find out that most reviews are actually negative).

If you already know what bloggers you want to contact, great! If you aren't sure, however, you may want to check out this article concerning the top 100 music blogs to follow in 2019 (https://blog.feedspot.com/music_blogs/). *Pitchfork*, the number one music blog has been at the top of the list for a while, but the odds that they will cover you as a new music streamer are low. It may be wise to start at the bottom of the list and check for bloggers that cover your genre and pick about ten to contact.

You should contact Vloggers as well, especially if you have a YouTube video to go with your song. Vloggers, especially those on YouTube, often have a large following and if you get them to say something positive about your song or video, many of their fans may check out your website. So, make sure that it is ready *even* if you are sending out an advanced copy of your song or video before it is actually released. Anyone who reviews your work may also want to check out your website; in fact, they may include other facts about you in their review.

You should contact music podcasts as well and as their hosts might decide to interview you. Being interviewed by a popular or even semi-popular podcast host can help you to attract the attention of listeners and hold it for a while so that you can tell them about yourself, the inspiration behind your music, and even have a chance to sing over the podcast. This is great publicity both before and after the release of a streaming single.

*Of course, it may be more effective to be featured on a few popular podcasts on the day of the release so that listeners that you have engaged can go to the streaming site and hear your music, supporting your release. Moreover, if they like it, they may add it to their playlists that day. And that mean more streams and a viral effect!*

One way to entice music bloggers, podcasters and vloggers is to promise them an exclusive song or video premiere. This means that for two or three days before the release date of your music, the only place that you can hear the new single or album is on the blogger's site or the podcast. If you have a following, this can help to drive viewers to the bloggers' website, podcast, or channel which increase their number of hits. Thus, it offers them a carrot of benefit to help bring some publicity to your music.

Make sure that you are polite and respectful when contacting these people. Also, make sure that you have your music and your bio ready to go. Your website site should be completed. Make a short pitch if contacting by email or mail. Provide information about the song and background information but do not bog them down in details. Also, you want to follow up if you do not hear from the person after a certain period of time. However, you do not want to be pushy or aggressive; it is better not to have your music reviewed than it is to royally piss a reviewer off. And you should respond to their responses ASAP!

# LOCAL COLLEGE RADIO

Yes, take a trip to your local college campus and see if you can get one of the radio hosts to interview you, let you sing on the air, mention you, or play your song. College students are the perfect age for streaming music platforms, and you will see many of them listening to streaming music from these services while walking to class. This means that this one place holds a ton of people who use streaming music platforms. Therefore, it does not matter if it is a community college, take a trip to as many colleges in your area as you can. This move could significantly increase your followers if you have a hit song. You can even place some flyers up on bulletin boards and in other places around the campus so that people can remember who you are and check out your music later. (At a college, you can even hand out flyers, stand on the quad and sing, ask a few people to listen to your song, and more.)

## PLAYLIST CURATORS

Yes, contacting playlist curators is a very important avenue to getting your songs on playlists. In fact, it is regarded as being so important that there are even services that will contact playlist curators for you to increase your chances of getting on their playlists. One such service is that of *Playlist Push*. Playlist Push will contact Spotify Playlist curators for you in the hopes of scoring you a spot on their playlist. Please, note that just as with any similar service, the results are not guaranteed and highly dependent on the track which you want to promote (*if you're interested in Playlist Push service, you may sign up with a 7,5% discount code "Z89MXJB", following this address: https://playlistpush.com*).

Contacting playlist curators may be a do-it-yourself move with the non-tastemaker curators, that aren't part of brands, and don't work for the streaming service. Some playlists by the average user have a significant number of followers. It is rather easy to find out the names and contact information of these playlist curators by going to the creator's homepage and contacting the curator through his or her social media links. This step will not, however, work for the higher tier playlist curators who receive too many requests from people to be added to their playlists.

One thing that you can do if you do not want to spend the money to have someone else contact the playlist curators for you is to search LinkedIn for their profiles (This applies to the on-staff Spotify curators who are supposedly all listed on LinkedIn). After finding their profiles on LinkedIn, check to see if there is any contact information there that you can use to get through. You could also try contacting them through other social media channels. However, there is a good chance that they may not respond.

You can type "contact playlist curators" into Google. You will not receive the email address of the playlist curators on the sites that come up, but many of them have ways to submit your music to Spotify playlist curators. This means

76

that you at least get to send a song in for consideration even if you don't get to send an email with it. Here is a short list of sites that let you contact independent playlist curators:

*http://indiemono.com/music-submit/*
*https://play.soundplate.com/*
*https://www.spingrey.com/backstage/*
*https://www.soaverecords.com/playlists*
*http://dailyplaylists.com/submit-a-track/*
*https://workhardplaylisthard.com/daily-beats-submissions*
*https://www.vgmandr.com/rizing-playlists.html*

Some sites offer to sell you the contact information of major playlist curators; be careful about using those sites. In fact, it is best not to. There are thousands of people submitting their songs to playlist curators and playlists every day. The contact information for this group of people would not be readily available to the public as they would receive too many calls and emails for them to have their information available to the public. So even if a service claims that it can get you the contact information for a fee, there is a good chance that you are just wasting your money. Sites that claim they will submit your songs to the curators, however, *may* be legitimate. However, you still need to be quite cautious when a site is asking you to pay a certain fee to submit your music to playlist curators (especially, if they "guarantee" your placement). As stated before, in order to battle these "guaranteed placements for a fee", Spotify has a new *free* submission tool which allows you to select one of your songs that have not been released and submit it to curated playlist for consideration.

# HOW TO CHOOSE PLAYLISTS

The best playlists are that in the same genre and niche area as your song so that it fits in well with the rest of the songs and the listeners. This is very important for your song to both have a legitimate chance of getting on the playlist as well as being played instead of skipped by most of the followers of the playlist. Make sure that your choice is both as targeted and as realistic as possible. Don't waste your submission trying to submit your new song to one of the 'Hits' playlists, especially if you are a newbie. It does not matter how hot you believe your song is. Trust me. Everyone believes that their song is hot enough to be on one of these playlists and almost none of the new songs by not-so-popular artists make it, at least not until the songs build up some traction and a number of followers.

## YOUR OWN CURATED PLAYLIST

You eventually want to become an influencer and not just an artist on the streaming music platforms to which you submit your music. Being an influencer gives you the opportunity to direct people to your music as well as the music of other artists that you like. This will give you a chance to present more of your music and get more streams.

Your own curated playlists should not just be a set of your songs unless you already have a significant number of followers. However, there are some great ways to attract followers to your playlist even if you do not already have a large group of followers.

### Create a Mood Based Playlist

Mood-based playlists are very popular and attract listeners based on the mood that they convey. Select a mood that matches several of your songs and add some well-known and quality songs from other artists that match that mood.

### Create an Activity Based Playlists

If your songs can go well with an activity, and streaming music platforms are not already saturated with playlists that cater to that activity, this could be a great niche area to target to gain followers quickly. (A tip – *Working Out* is an area that is typically <u>completely</u> saturated with playlists. Try to choose something unique so that your playlist won't have a great deal of competition.)

*Create A Regional or Local Playlist*

You can create a playlist with some from artists in your local area and even put up flyers around town to advertise the playlist and draw people to it. Try to select an area where you can get a significant number of followers. However, do not target an area that is too big or not attractive for people. (You may even want to try to get your local playlist mentioned on local radio.)

/12/2017 — 5/25/2017

210,000

180,000

150,000

essions

,811

5.05%

Avg. daily viewers

115,945

6%

# CHAPTER 7

# TRACKING OF RESULTS

T racking music releases metrics has become so important in this day and age of streaming music services that it has turned into a multi-million-dollar industry with many powerful players getting in on it. Companies such as MusicMetric, Charmetric etc, are popping up to measure the success of tracks that were once gauged by radio play, CD sales, and downloads. In fact, some of these companies eventually get acquired by the biggest streaming networks. Spotify acquired The Echo Nest, a music metrics system to help it keep track of the success of tracks on its music streaming service. The aforementioned MusicMetric was acquired by Apple.

Of course, big-name artist have designated teams tracking all of their music metrics from a number of different angles and spending a great deal of money to do this. But you, as a new and up and coming artist may not have the resources to track all of your metrics like a pro. There are still some ways that you can track the success of your release and some affordable tools that you can use to see how your release is measuring up and where there is room for advancement and improvement.

## WHERE TO GET YOUR DATA: INFORMATION SOURCES

If you submit your music through a digital distributor, this digital distributor often keeps track of many of the important metrics for you. Thus, if you are simply a musician and want to concentrate on your art without having to know how to do much of the number-work behind the scenes, it may be better for you to spend the extra money to submit your work through a digital distributor which provides such statistics in an easy-to-digest format (just to name a few: CDBaby, TuneCore, Ditto Music, LANDR, RouteNote). Most of the time, this data from your distributor may be enough to judge about the success of your release.

However, if you wish to really track your campaign with the right level of detail, out of many tools that can help you, one of the most advanced is **Chartmetric** (https://chartmetric.io). Chartmetric claims to be a modern data tool for the streaming age and it is so. It offers comprehensive and customizable music analytics, tracking 1.3 million artists, 1 million playlists, and 300K curators across Spotify, Apple Music, and Deezer. If you want to understand your release success, this is a great tool for you to have so that you do not have to try to add up all of the numbers on your own. The service lays out the information very clearly in an organized manner so that you can understand it without additional help. There are various tiers for pro clients, but the free tier typically provides enough data an indie artist.

Furthermore, this tool will give you additional information that may not be considered a metric but can still give you an advantage when it comes to deciding what course of action you should take next to promote your music even further. One example of this is *curator ranking*. You can find out what curators are ranked the highest and what music industry tastemakers have the biggest following so that you can make a better decision on who to contact.

# WHAT TO TRACK

### PLAYLISTS AND PLAYLIST RANKINGS

Getting on playlists, although it should not be the only metric that an artist takes into account, is your primary starting point. As we discussed before playlists do possess great power. According to Digital Music News, getting on some top-ranked playlists can literally transform your career overnight. So much so that, *"those who disregard the power of the playlist may be playing with their careers. An artist that places well on playlists can expect bigger crowds at shows, better sales of vinyl and merch, and even juicy sync advertising and collaboration deals"* ("Playlists Aren't Everything. Here Are Some Other Critical Metrics to Track an Artist's Success", *Digital Music News* by Paul Resnikoff).

Therefore, whether or not your releases have made it onto playlists is your first key measure of success. The number of playlists that a track is on helps to illustrate how the users of the platform have received the track.

## Curated (Editorial) Playlists

Where a song has made it onto a curated (editorial) playlist is definitely an important sign to look at. Making it onto these playlists helps to show that industry tastemakers respect your music. The average user of music streaming services may know what he or she likes and listen to what is trending; however, the curators judge the music by its quality and its potential for commercial success. This means that if a track has made it onto a curated playlist, it has received the industry nod of approval, at least from one tastemaker.

*Playlist Ranking*

However it is not simply whether or not your music has made it onto curated playlists that matters. In addition to the type of playlist that the song has made it onto, it is important to look at whether the playlist is a high-ranking playlist or just an average playlist. If the playlists that you are on aren't ranked in the highest tiers in the streaming music platforms on which you loaded the songs, there is still room for improvement. Don't lose the momentum! Try contacting bloggers and curators again, and this time provide them with the information about how well your songs are doing and what playlists they are *already on* to see if you can get on more playlists.

In addition to the number of followers that a playlist has, it is important for you to note the activity of the playlist. Do the playlist's followers listen to the playlist every day? Is the playlist in high rotation? Is the playlist experiencing growth? Newer playlists may not have as many followers as some of the more established playlist, but the numbers for these lists may be growing at a faster rate. It is very important to examine this trend when looking at the playlist's quality because it may be a bit easier for you to get songs into playlists which have a growing number of followers than it is to get your songs on playlists which *already* have a big number of followers.

## STREAMS AND OTHER RELATED METRICS

The number of streams that a song receives is another important metric to gauge your success. In fact, many consider it to be the number one indicator. However, there is no set number of streams that determines whether or not the release was a success. Spotify shows the number of plays a song received after it has gotten to at least 1,000. Thus, this has to be the *bare minimum* for the song to have made any impact at all.

It is also important to note that it takes approximately 180,0p00 streams for an artist to make minimum wage in the United States from streaming music. Thus, if streaming music is what you plan do for a living, you should want to achieve at least twice that many. And for a song to be considered a commercial success for the industry, the number of plays must be in the millions.

Now, let's talk about your *followers*. To be considered a moderate success on social media platforms when

87

promoting yourself, you need to have approximately 2,500 to 5,000 followers (this is a number of real followers, engaged with your music and not 'accidental' ones). A successful social media presence requires over 5,000 followers, and highly successful social media pages typically have 10,000 and up for streaming music artists. These are the numbers for typical social media platforms. But what about your *artist page followers*? On Spotify, your follower numbers may mean at least something if you managed to attract pretty much the same numbers – 2,000-3,000 followers (again, we're not talking about those 'purchased' fake followers, but your real fans). These followers get informed by Spotify when you release your new singles/albums and they also have higher chances of being recommended your tracks when they use the 'add recommended songs' feature of the platform, when creating playlists in your genre.

Yet, the number of followers does not <u>guarantee</u> your plays. Thus, next to the number of followers, another metric which you need to take into account is your *'monthly listeners'* number. This number is typically much bigger than your followers. If an artist is in the active growing phase on the platform, the number of monthly listeners will show you consistent growth as well.

So, to sum up, in order to understand how well your tracks perform on the streaming platform, you want to monitor the number/ranking of playlists your songs are on, the dynamics of your followers' growth as well as the dynamics of your monthly listeners.

### SOUNDCLOUD FOLLOWERS

Another key metric that is used to measure the success of an artist and his or her release is that of SoundCloud followers. The primary reason cited for placing focus on Soundcloud followers is that this streaming music platform offers a higher level of engagement allowing you to tell the difference between a simple *like* button click and an actual fan who is really connected with your music.

In fact, having a strong following on Soundcloud can help to catapult you to success on other streaming music platforms such as Spotify and Apple Music. Soundcloud Rap is cited for catapulting stars such as the late *XXXTentacion* and *Lil Peep* to stardom. Another major example of how success on Soundcloud can turn into success in real life is *Post Malone;* he started off with one smash single on SoundCloud, now has a total of 1.2 million followers on this music service, a figure that will make the who's who of the rap industry stand up and take notice. Another example is *Billie Eilish* who

89

was signed to Universal Music Group after her success on SoundCloud.

### A *Shazam* ID & *Shazam* Spikes

Shazam is a service that identifies any music that is playing around the user. Thus, if your song is streaming, being played on the radio, being played in a store, or is being played in a television show, someone can use Shazam to find out more information about the track such as the name of the song and the artist. This typically shows that people liked the song, it caught their attention, and that they would like to hear it again.

Shazam used to be really hot when downloads were the most popular way to listen to music, but this service has not fallen off yet. It is considered by some in the industry to be an influencer, letting the tastemakers in the industry know what songs people are searching for and want to hear. According to Digital Music News, if a track has a Shazam ID, this typically indicates significant interest in a track. Thus, you may want to check Shazam and see if your track have an ID so you can gauge exactly how much people may be searching for your tracks. Check out Shazam at https://www.shazam.com.

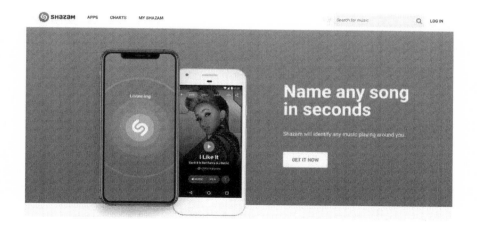

## AUDIENCE DENSITY IN A GIVEN LOCALE

Audience density in a given locale is another indicator of the success of a track, on a local, citywide, or regional level. This is an important metric if you would like to determine where it would be best for you to schedule any live performances. In fact, checking out audience density can help you to access the demographic better that most likes your music so that you can generate and maintain a core fan base. This metric can help you to determine where your fans are city goers, suburbanites, or Midwesterners so that you can tailor your releases to this group of people. Typically, digital distributors offer this sort of metric as part of their basic post-release analysis data.

## ARTIST PROFILE

Many people may not realize that not only your Spotify followers should be watched and monitored during your campaigns, but also your entire social media artist footprint. *Chartmetric* allows you to monitor your artist profile and check it against other artists to see how well you are doing in this area. You can see the growth of all of your social media platforms and it is another important indicator of the success of your release. Gaining more Instagram, Twitter, Facebook, SnapChat followers and more can be a sign that fans liked your music and decided to follow you to see what you are doing outside of the streaming music platform. I will repeat myself here, but this is another reason why you should make sure that *all of your social media accounts are up to date and ready before your release* and *listed to your artist page on the streaming music sites*. If your number of followers jumps up across all of your social media platforms, this is a definite sign of success, and it also helps you build a foundation for more mainstream success.

## UPLOADS TO YOUTUBE

You should track both official and unofficial uploads to YouTube. Even if you have to ask someone later to take down your music or music video due to a copyright violation because you only want it up on your channel, the fact that

92

someone took the time to upload it shows that it is liked and may have sufficient popularity. I mean, back in the time the most popular songs were the ones most pirated on Napster!

Furthermore, if you are submitting a video to YouTube, you can see how many views you received. This is very important to keep track of if you want to start making money on YouTube through ad revenue. Also, keep track of the followers on your YouTube channel. Both of these figures can allow you to make revenue through advertisements being placed in that video or a number of videos.

## PHYSICAL & DIGITAL PURCHASES

Even in the streaming music era, the volume of downloads of a song or album as well as the physical sale of CDs still is an important metric to look at. In fact, looking at this metric can tell you more about the popularity of an individual song than the number of plays that it receives on a streaming music site. This is because those who take the time to go over to a site like Amazon.com or iTunes and buy the song are more interested in that song specifically instead of a group of songs that are on a playlist. Furthermore, this shows that your fans are really engaged and that they are actually willing to spend some of their hard-earned money to acquire your music. This is a very important metric that you want to show promoters and club owners if you would like to start performing shows.

## TRADITIONAL RADIO AIRPLAY

The streaming platforms can let you know if your tracks have the potential for commercial success. However, the radio is still a very good indicator of whether a song is a commercial success. With radio success, you can get music synced to television, advertisements, and in movies and these are great sources of income and exposure. Thus, it is not only success on the streaming platforms that an artist should look at when he or she releases a song on a streaming platform.

## SYNC DEALS

Yes, you do want to make your music available for sync deals, and this is a very good alternative source of income. Music is often used in advertisements, on television, and in movies and these deals, called sync deals, may also get you additional exposure. Furthermore, if you approach a record label after making your release and tracking it for a while on streaming media channels, it would be a great asset to you to be able to say that one of your songs was used in a major advertisement, on a television show, or in a movie. This helps to add some legitimacy to your work and show that it is commercially ready. So be sure to check with the digital distributor and keep a record of whether any syncs were done.

## MUSIC BLOGGERS

As we discussed before, paying attention to music blogs offers a great way to find out what music experts think about new releases. This is especially true if you can get one of them to review your music or at least comment on it. Thus, if you tried contacting music bloggers as part of your release marketing campaign, you may want to contact them again after your other metrics start to show a successful release. Bloggers will be more likely to respond and cover your music again if the audience reacts to it positively.

## BEATPORT

Beatport is a service that radio and club DJs use to purchase higher quality downloads which they can play in the club or on the radio. If your songs (or remixes) are being played by DJs in clubs, you will be able to find this out by checking to see how many times they have been downloaded on Beatport.

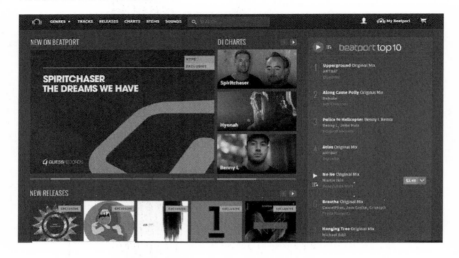

# CHAPTER 8

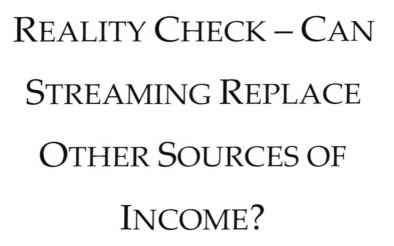

# REALITY CHECK – CAN STREAMING REPLACE OTHER SOURCES OF INCOME?

S o, here is a reality check – with the millions of songs that are available on streaming services and the vast number of artists and musicians who are submitting music to these services every day, it is rather unlikely that you will make enough money through music streaming *only*. Even if you follow all of the strategies and tactics outlined in this book.

Even if you get placement on some of the popular playlists, you may simply receive more income from your music than you would have if you had not been on a playlist. And this income may disappear once the buzz around your latest release gets lower.

However if you build up your name, your following, and treat your music as a systemic business project – the streaming income will turn from a side income, which you may only notice if you get accidentally *lucky*, to a reliable additional income source which is a part of your music business strategy (I have discussed this strategy in my first book: "MY MUSIC – MY BUSINESS" and I hope you had a chance to read it).

Streaming music gives you an avenue to be heard and build up a following. It allows you a chance to get your name out there for those of you who are trying to break into the music industry. But after you have gotten your foot in the door, you want to follow up with traditional recording artist activities such as performing in shows, getting syncing deals with television and movies, selling music and merchandise and more.

Thus, sending you music to streaming music providers and getting on playlists can be a great way for you to *open up* other avenues of income through your music. Gauging the success of your release can open the door for you to live shows. You may be able to sell some merchandise, especially to your streaming music followers. You definitely should be able to sell more MP3 which provides the artist with more money per sale that streaming music does per play. In addition, you ought to be able to be able to sell a few CDs or vynil copies of your releases as well. Songwriters should receive royalties form radio play. Be sure to take advantage of **every avenue to making money with your music that you can** after you submit the music to streaming music services.

What can you expect from streaming services in the future? I expect that they will undoubtedly come up with more ways for artists (and streaming platforms) to *make more money* in order to keep a steady flow of quality songs coming in. There is a lot of innovation resources being pulled into this industry right now and we should see new features and possibilities to be available for both users and artists quite soon. Thus, even if the answer to "whether you can have a sustainable, money-making career as an artist *only* through streaming music now" is *probably not*, in the near future, there is a good chance that the answer will change. Thus, it is important for you to stay ahead of the tide of people submitting music to streaming services and treat your music streaming activities as part of your strategic music business plan.

# CHAPTER 9

# THE FUTURE OF STREAMING AND YOUR STREAMING RELEASE STRATEGIES

## STREAMING SERVICES = RECORD COMPANIES

Although major recording artists are still turning a significant profit in the new age of music streaming, there is still a standing complaint that streaming music has made it difficult for a less well-known artist to make a profit. Due to these complaints, you need to be prepared to see some changes in the way that digital service providers or streaming music companies provide service in upcoming years. There is a suggestion that the biggest streaming music services such as Spotify, Apple Music act as *record companies* that represent selected artists who place music on their platforms. This can help the artist make more money when you consider the fact that record companies often take as much as 70% of the payout for each song put out by artists on their label.

## EXCLUSIVE DEALS FOR STREAMING STARS

Major stars such as *Chance The Rapper* can already sign deals with major music streaming services and offer their music exclusively to that particular music streaming platform for a limited amount of time. This is not a unique case, however. Therefore, as more and more people become *"streaming music"* stars by putting out their music right out of their home studio without the backing of a record label, streaming services *may* begin to offer these artists exclusive deals even if they are not household names. Artists should pay attention to all of the new options that streaming music services will begin to offer to get quality artists and music on their platform so that they can be the first to get in these deals.

In fact, in mid-2018 Spotify made a commitment to independent artists through non-exclusive licensing agreements. These agreements will compensate the artists who receive them with advances that can be thousands if not tens of thousands of dollars for agreeing to license a certain number of songs *directly* to the platform (i.e. instead of using third-party distribution services). These agreements do not require that the songs be exclusively provided to Spotify. *You must try to get one of these deals if you can!*

## THE RISE AND FALL OF STREAMING SERVICES

As you know, Spotify is the biggest streaming network at this moment. However it's possible that other streaming services may close the gap in the coming year. Apple Music is the one which you need to closely monitor – its subscriber base was 57 million at years end (vs. 87 million of Spotify). Even though the service is less advanced in terms of the range/quality of services offered to its subscribers, Apple may still show significant growth in the upcoming years. As an artist, you have to make sure to monitor the competition closely to benefit from all those exciting new competitive features which may soon appear on these streaming platforms (especially those which are related to such services as artist promotion, interaction with listeners etc).

## SMART SPEAKERS AND PLAYLISTS

Even if you don't have a smart speaker at home, the market reality is that they are here to stay. Their penetration has been growing consistently year on year and their mass adoption is only a question of time. Amazon is currently the biggest player in this segment, occupying 68% market share. Thus, you may expect that Amazon Music Unlimited adoption is also going to increase. Given the ongoing technological revolution, it's a good idea to monitor the state of your streaming activity on Amazon's streaming platform and try to identify ways of including this network in your future music expansion business plan.

# CONCLUSION

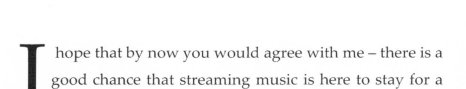

I hope that by now you would agree with me – there is a good chance that streaming music is here to stay for a long time. This is the primary reason that this book title includes the *'streaming revolution'* term!

Streaming music has revolutionized the music industry, and even with all of the complaints that artists have about not being paid enough for their music, streaming music has solved the problem of consumers 'stealing' the music altogether through illegal downloads, sharing downloads, copying CDs and more (in fact, Spotify came out of Sweden - one of the countries with the highest level of piracy!). So, on the bright side, at least artists are getting paid every time their song is played on a streaming platform, even if the amount is less than they would have hoped.

The digital streaming revolution has transformed the access of musicians to their listeners. Now everybody who can release high quality music, has a chance to build up a large fan base and create a sustainable music business. This was impossible in the past, when record labels were functioning as 'gateways' into the world of music business.

And there are a number of streaming music platforms which new entrants can choose from all which have slightly different features. Spotify, one of the lowest paying per stream platforms actually has the most users which add to your total number of streams. Apple Music offers a higher payout to artists. Deezer is primarily for artists outside of the United States. Google Play allows you to decide if and how you want to sell your songs for a chance at a higher payout. And SoundCloud offers greater artist/fan interaction and a chance to really make it big like *Post Malone*.

Digital distributors can help you satisfy all distribution requirements and get your music in all of the right places. And a great marketing plan can help to get your songs noticed. Once again, if you are serious about your music – do not underestimate the need to have a properly planned marketing and advertising/promotion plan!

So the next step is to take all these tips and go out and *CREATE.* I wish you best of luck and major success with your next release!

Finally, I really hope you enjoyed this book and if you happen to have any feedback – please, do not hesitate to leave a few words with your impressions on Amazon. I am extremely grateful for your feedback and will also gladly take your advice for potential future subjects of **"MY MUSIC – MY BUSINESS"** series.

You can reach me at: *tim@musicmybusiness.com*

Thank you!

\* \* \*

**TIM SIVERS**

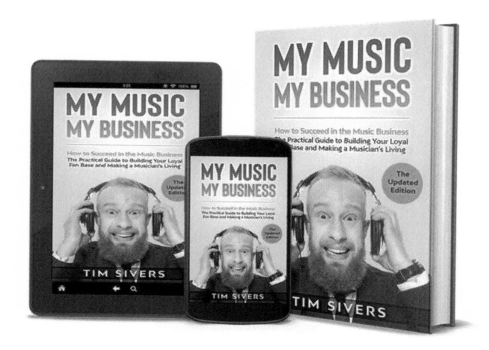

# BONUS

*AS A SPECIAL **THANK YOU** FOR YOUR PURCHASE, I HAVE
PREPARED A VERY SPECIAL PRESENT FOR YOU.
I WOULD LIKE TO OFFER YOU THE 1ST BOOK IN THE "MY MUSIC –
MY BUSINESS" SERIES ABSOLUTELY FOR **FREE**.
PLEASE, FOLLOW THE LINK BELOW TO DOWNLOAD YOUR COPY:*

## http://bit.ly/MyMusicMyBusinessFREE

*(PLEASE, NOTE THAT THE CAPITALIZATION OF WORDS IN THE LINK
IS IMPORTANT)*

Made in the USA
Middletown, DE
14 March 2019